Erratum

The publishers regret that the
photograph taken at Glendalough
on page 199 has appeared in error
in the Millennium chapter.

TRANSWORLD PUBLISHERS LTD
61 – 63 Uxbridge Road, London W5 5SA

TRANSWORLD PUBLISHERS (AUSTRALIA) PTY LTD
15 – 23 Helles Avenue, Moorebank NSW 2170

TRANSWORLD PUBLISHERS (NZ) LTD
Cnr Moselle and Waipareira Aves,
Henderson, Auckland

Published 1988 by Bantam Press,
a division of Transworld Publishers Ltd
Copyright © Irish Cancer Society 1988
Designed by Associated Design Consultants, London
Typeset by Lazy Dog, London
Colour reproduction by Alpha Reprographics, Perivale
Printed in West Germany by
Mohndruck Graphische Betriebe GmbH, Gütersloh

British Library Cataloguing in Publication Data

One day for life in Ireland.
1. Ireland. Social life
941.50824

ISBN 0-593-01641-6

Contents

Gay Byrne
CRONA AND SUZY WITH DAD

Foreword

Saturday, May 7th, 1988 was a very special day in Ireland when
thousands of people all over the country celebrated life and
captured it on film.

This book *One Day for Life in Ireland* records what the people of
Ireland did on that day. The photographs are remarkable for
their quality and capture the spirit of the Irish nation.

One in four people in Ireland develop cancer and one in seven
die of cancer. This book is for all those who are still fighting, to
encourage them and to thank them for their inspiration.
I would also like to say a word of thanks to doctors, scientists,
nurses and volunteers for their dedicated care of
cancer patients.

This book is for all of us because all of us at some stage in our
lives will be touched by cancer.

Dr GAY BYRNE
Patron of One Day for Life in Ireland

Early morning in a city has a very special atmosphere. Bernice Abbot
suggested that Eugene Adjet's wonderful photographs of Paris repeatedly
suggest the stage setting which one beholds after the curtain goes up.
My photograph of James Gandon's masterpiece, the Four Courts, has a
timeless quality, broken only by the lorry parked to the left of the picture.

ROBERT BALLAGH

The EARLY HOURS

12.00-6.00

Mr David Monahan
NIGHT LIFE: O'CONNELL STREET
12.10am: Westmoreland Street,
Dublin

John Mullins
TWENTY-FOUR-HOUR BANKING
2.00am: South Mall, Cork

Brendan Lawlor
HOTEL KILKENNY
3.25am: Kilkenny

Stephen St Legér: Age 17
LEANING ON LAMP-POST,
GRAFTON STREET
4.00am: Grafton Street, Dublin

Anne Marie Walker
HOWTH HEAD
5.30am: Poolbeg Lighthouse,
Dublin (Front cover photograph)

Ken Dobson
MAN WITH GREYHOUNDS
6.00am: South Strand, Skerries,
Co. Dublin

Stephen St Legér: Age 17
HA'PENNY BRIDGE
4.00am: Ha'penny Bridge, Dublin

Facing page:
Matt Gahan
RIVER BARROW AT SUNRISE
6.00am: River Barrow,
New Ross, Co. Wexford

Frederick Snowe
DESPATCH ROOM *IRISH TIMES*
4.10am: D'Olier Street, Dublin

Mr William O'Brien
SPIDER'S WEB
6.00am: Galbally, Co. Tipperary

Mr Michael Corrigan
DAWN ON THE BURREN
6.00am: The Burren, Co. Clare

Peter Cavanagh
GETTING READY FOR THE DAY
5.45am: Dun Laoghaire, Co. Dublin

Pádraig Kennelly
DAWN
6.15am: Caragh Lake, Co. Kerry

Jonathan Redmond: Age 14
EARLY START
6.15am: Grand Canal, Dublin

Dawn begins with a breakfast of mice for these young kestrels. The nest is a
ruin shared by several families of jackdaws who all seem to have benefited
from the Norman Conquest. The kestrel is one of our commonest birds of prey
and its habit of hanging in mid-air with quivering wings and depressed tail
has given it the name 'Wind-hover'.

ÉAMON DE BUITLÉAR

'End of Another Season': This weekend marks the end of yet another erratic
year in Irish Rugby during which nothing was simply 'Black and White'!
All that's left now are the memories of games played, of new friendships made
and of old friendships cemented. Roll on next September when the gates will
open once again to usher in a new season and dreams of what might be.

We have a race to run,
We have a job that must be done,
Only we have the power to achieve,
Courage and effort will see us
*   through,*
And give us freedom to plan our
*   own lives,*
And realise our dreams.

OLLIE CAMPBELL

The
MORNING

6.00-10.00

Angela MacMahon
BATHTIME FUN
9.00am: Killiney, Co. Dublin

Nora Lalor
NIAMH BLOWING BUBBLES
9.15am: Clondalkin, Dublin

Amanda Loughran
THE NEW EUROPEAN BREED
9.30am: Dalkey, Co. Dublin

Mr Jeremy Henehan
RECRUITS UNDER TRAINING
9.30am: Naval Base, Haulbowline,
Co. Cork

Mr Michael Morris
'ATTITUDE ADJUSTER'
9.30am: Fethard, Co. Tipperary

Facing page:
Mr Andy Murray
SHEENA'S COMMUNION DAY
9.30am: Ashbourne, Co. Meath

Mr John Ellison
ST KEVIN'S CHURCH AND
ROUND TOWER
9.30am: Glendalough, Co. Wicklow

Mr Philip Murphy
FOUR MINUTES AFTER HIS FIRST
COMMUNION
9.45am: Dublin

Mrs J.N. King
FERMOY CHAMPIONSHIP
DOG SHOW
9.50am: Fermoy, Co. Cork

Mr Con M. Conner
OLD SCHOOL MANCH ESTATE
9.01am: Manch, Ballineen, Co. Cork

Eileen O'Connor: Age 12
KIDS GETTING ON TOP OF YOU?
9.00am: El-Rancho, Tralee,
Co. Kerry

Mrs C. Moulder
IT'S JIM SEERY HOLDING ON
9.40am: Beresford Place, Dublin

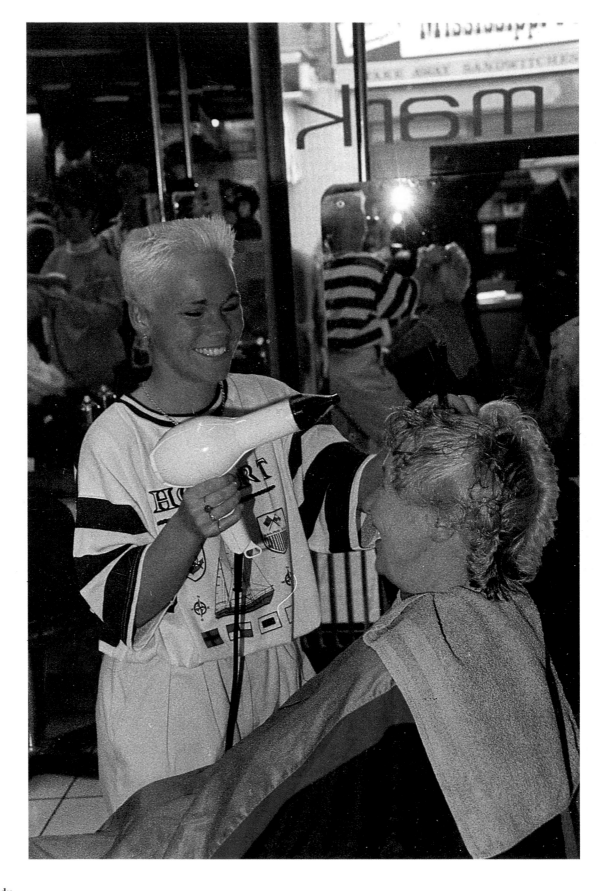

E. A. Kennedy
WEEKEND HAIRDO
9.30am: Ilac Centre, Dublin

8.00am: The woods at Cloch mo Choda Killarney.

Early in the morning … bright sunshine … the richest colours imaginable …
bluebells, hawthorn, hazel … my daughter Audrey and pet owl Snowy …
the humming quietness of nature: surely this is heaven on earth.

PAT O'CONNELL

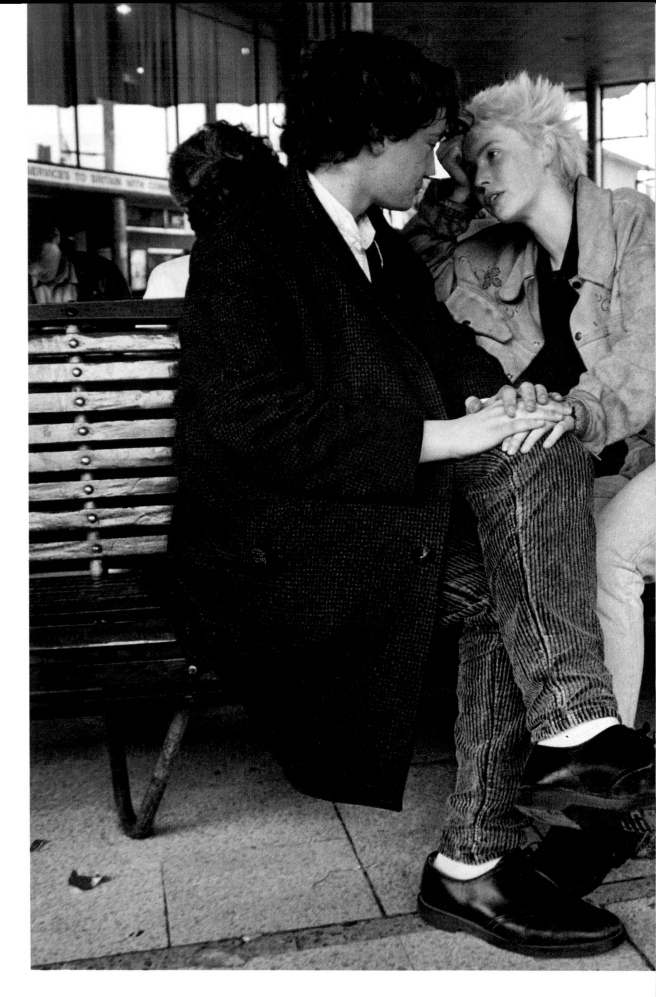

Mr Michael Johnson
NEARLY TIME TO PART
10.00am: Busarus, Dublin

58

Finola Hand
LOBSTER FISHING DINGLE BAY
10.00am: Bull's Head, Kinard,
Co. Kerry

Father Stephen Farragher
IRELAND'S TRAVELLING PEOPLE
10.15am: Gilmartin Road, Tuam,
Co. Galway

Adrienne Gilmartin
A CHILD'S VIEW
11.00am: Marley Park, Dublin

Mr Joe Fleming
BOATS TO THE ISLAND
11.00am: Coliemore Harbour,
Dalkey

Facing page:
Mr David Morrison
CAT O' NINE MILES
10.30am: Knockanore, Co. Waterford

EOCHAILL 9
YOUGHAL

MOR MOCHUDA
SMORE 9

CNOC AN ÓIR
KNOCKANORE

CEAPACH CHOINN
CAPPOQUIN 9

TULACH AN IARAINN
TALLOW 9

Colm Henry
FIRST COMMUNION
10.30am: Inchicore Church, Dublin

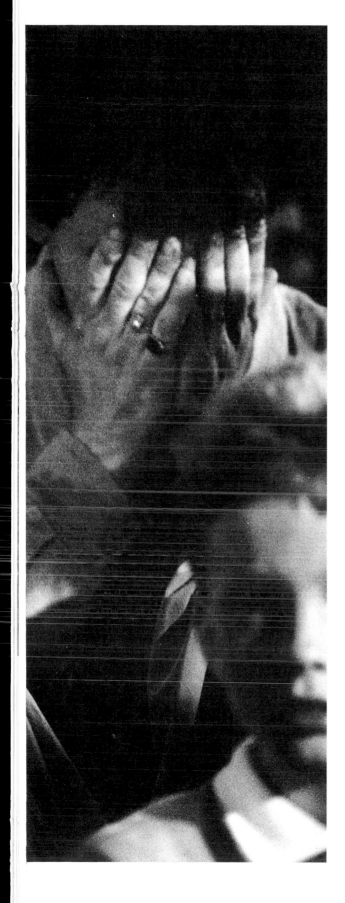

Geraldine Daly
GO NO FURTHER!
10.00am: Shelbourne Park,
Limerick

Paddy Prior
CASUAL TRADING AREA
10.30am: Thurles, Co. Tipperary

Mrs Anne Towers
DAVID AND GOLIATHS
12.00 noon: Askeaton, Co. Limerick

Marcus MacInnes: Age 16
FEEDING THE DUCKS
12.00 noon: St Stephen's Green,
Dublin. (Winning photograph
Under-18's)

Facing page:
Mr Terry Murphy
BLOWING ONE DAY FOR
LIFE TROPHY
11.40am: Waterford Crystal Ltd.
Kilbarry, Co. Waterford

Mr Patsy Conway
WAITING FOR BUYERS
1.00pm: Ballinasloe Market,
Co. Galway

Briga O'Connell
STUDY OF A STUDIOUS BOY
1.00pm: Annaghdown, Co.
Galway

Rev. Michael J. McKeon
ON YOUR HEAD BE IT
1.00pm: Crossna Church,
Co. Roscommon

Mr Matt Gahan
BISHOP OF FERNS AND FRIENDS
1.00pm: St Aidan's Cathedral,
Enniscorthy, Co. Wexford

Echoes of rapturous laughter ...
Cherry blossom tumbling on pathways ...

Dublin sparkled in the sunlight,
*   and carefree hearts were bent on play.*
An empty playground became a noisy wonderland.
A big blue ball was bounced and thrown and
*   breathlessly retrieved.*
Little fingers stroked the glossy black hearts
*   of red tulips.*
Secure in love, their world was golden.

My heart filled with love, a pure selflessness.
What would life do to them?

Already that day has the delicate scent of
*   lavender.*
It's a treasured memory.

MARY FINAN

Jim Masterson
FRANCES MORAN: ARTIST
2.30pm: Pembroke Road, Dublin

Paul Mulvany
THE CURIOSITY SHOP
2.35pm: Market Lane, Cork

Michael Bloor
DONKEY AND FOAL
2.15pm: Near Mulrany, Co. Mayo

Mr J. Chandler
TIMES THEY ARE A'CHANGING
3.00pm: Ennis Market-place,
Co. Clare

Mary O'Neill-Byrne
FRIENDS WITH SIDE-CAR
3.00pm. Rathnew, Co. Wicklow

Patrick Reilly
KATY AND SUZANNE
3.00pm: Ballymakenny Road,
Drogheda

Facing page:
Denis Whelehan
GIRL IN RED DRESS
4.00pm: Carrick Road, Dundalk

Mr Thomas Sunderland
MUSICIANS, TULLOW STREET
4.00pm: Tullow Street, Carlow

Brendan Buggy
CURIOSITY
4.30pm: Bull Island, Co. Dublin

Josephine Roche
CRUINNIÚ FAOIN MBÁD
3.00pm: Roundstone Library,
Co. Galway

J. Craig McKechnie
A KERRY GOAT
4.00pm: Sneam,
Co. Kerry

Maria Brady
SMILE PLEASE
4.00pm: Beech Park, Lucan,
Co. Dublin

Mona O'Moore
READY FOR WIMBLEDON?
3.30pm: Sandycove, Co. Dublin

Robert C. Hayden
TRADITIONAL BUTCHERS
3.05pm: Main Street, Kinsale,
Co. Cork

Stephanie Condon
SHARON AND RONAN DOYLE
3.00pm: Dalkey Island Hotel,
Co. Dublin

Mr Ken Trimble
EIGHTY YEARS A-GROWING
3.30pm: Ballyconeely, Co. Galway

James Murray
PENALTY RUSH
3.00pm: St Mark's Senior School,
Tallaght, Co. Dublin

James Hynes
CHILDREN ON THE BEACH
4.00pm: Portmarnock Beach,
Co. Dublin

Tom Raftery
BLUEBELLS AND BEECH TREES
3.30pm: Boyle,
Co. Roscommon

Tony Clarke
IT'S A COVERUP
3.00pm: Beenbawn, Dingle,
Co. Kerry

Facing page:
Trevor Looney: Age 16
HOLD ON AND LET GO!
2.30pm: Mornington Avenue, Trim,
Co. Meath

Declan Nevin
FULL STEAM AHEAD
4.15pm: Marley Park, Dublin

Mary B. Kelly
JERRY KISSES THE BLARNEY STONE
3.45pm: Blarney Castle, Blarney,
Co. Cork

Fionnuala Molloy
CANAL IN TULLAMORE
3.20pm: Belmount Lock, Tullamore

Brian Ó Carra
DOING THE CONNEMARA SET
3.00pm: Renvyle, Co. Galway

128

Hugh Frazer
AFTERNOON AT SHANKILL RIVER
3.00pm: Near Kilbride,
Co. Wicklow

Noel Murphy
PROUD BOY
4.00pm: Ballymascanlon, Dundalk

Jerry Kennelly
GARDA JIM
3.45pm: Cahirciveen, Co. Kerry

Mr Gerry Bracken
MARTHA'S BIG DAY
3.00pm: Westport, Co. Mayo

Mrs Mary Lee
LAMB ON THE BOTTLE
3.00pm: Keane's Farm, Loughrea,
Co. Galway

Lorraine Gannon
DINNY AT THE CLIFFS
5.15pm: Cliffs of Moher, Co. Clare

Maurice Coyle
JAMIE'S REWARD ON THE WAY
5.30pm: McDonald's, Dun Laoire,
Co. Dublin

Mary Bruton
SWEETSELLER AT THE RACES
5.00pm: Leopardstown Race
Course, Co. Dublin

Mrs E. McMahon
NO MORE PHOTOS, MUMMY!
5.00pm: Granville Road, Killiney,
Co. Dublin

Tim O'Sullivan
HANDS OFF, IT'S MINE!
5.00pm: Paul Street, Cork

Ignatius O'Neill
THE BLUEBELL GIRL
5.15pm: Jenkinstown Wood,
near Kilkenny

Matt Gahan
SHEEP FARMING ON
MOUNT LEINSTER
5.30pm: Mount Leinster

Mrs P. Stanley
SPRING EVENING
6.00pm: Gougane Barra, Co. Cork

Suzanne Donnelly: Age 16
WISE AND SIMPLE MEN
3.30pm: Balbriggan Harbour,
Co. Dublin

Aodhán McBreen
SUMMER AT LAST
3.30pm: Drumeague, Bailieborough,
Co. Cavan

Kay O'Sullivan
LIGHTENING THE LOAD
6.00pm: Drom, Templemore,
Co. Tipperary

Noreen Walshe-Harte
TONES OF SUMMER REPOSE
6.00pm: Cill Rónaín, Aran Islands

Mr H.W. Pearce
EVENING AT KYLEMORE ABBEY
6.00pm: Kylemore Abbey,
Co. Galway

John D. Killeen
RUTH MULLEADY'S FAVOURITE
IRISH MUSIC
8.00pm: Booterstown, Co. Dublin

Francis Chambers
LOUGH ENNEL
7.45pm: Lough Ennel,
Co. Westmeath

Noreen Walshe-Harte
TONES OF SUMMER REPOSE
6.00pm: Cill Rónaín, Aran Islands

Mr H.W. Pearce
EVENING AT KYLEMORE ABBEY
6.00pm: Kylemore Abbey,
Co. Galway

Ellen Duggan
PUPPY LOVE
6.00pm: Ussory Lodge, Dunmore,
Co. Kilkenny

Mrs R. Moulder
RYAN'S BEDTIME PADDLE
WITH GRANDAD
6.30pm: Spanish Point, Co. Clare

Sean Slevin
IRISH COTTAGE
6.53pm: Knockavilla, New Ross,
Co. Wexford

Breda Flannery
FIRE-EATING DONKEY
6.45pm: Ballycommon, Menagh,
Co. Tipperary

Mrs Monique Bolger
WASHED OUT
7.00pm: Spiddal, Co. Galway

Peter O'Kennedy
TOWER CAFÉ
7.00pm: Sandymount, Co. Dublin

Mrs Geraldine Downey
FOOTPRINTS IN THE SAND
7.00pm: Lahinch

Kevin P. Leonard
MEMORIES OF CLONGOWES
7.00pm: Clongowes

Francis O'Neill
WHAT'S DADDY DOING UP THERE?
7.15pm: Brian Road, Marino,
Dublin

Pádraig Ó Flannabhra
FLANNERY FAMILY, URRA-HILL
7.15pm: Urra-Hill, Nenagh,
Co. Tipperary

Martin O'Sullivan
SLAKING THE THIRST
7.20pm: Main Street, Schull,
Co. Cork

John D. Killeen
RUTH MULLEADY'S FAVOURITE
IRISH MUSIC
8.00pm: Booterstown, Co. Dublin

Francis Chambers
LOUGH ENNEL
7.45pm: Lough Ennel,
Co. Westmeath

Tom Campbell
DO YOU COME HERE OFTEN?
8.00pm: Lough Lannagh,
Castlebar, Co. Mayo

Liam O'Sullivan
HOPE BEYOND THE
DARKENED DOOR
8.00pm: Lady's Abbey, near
Ardfinnan, Clonmel

Matt Gahan
JAUNTING CART AT
KILLARNEY LAKES
8.15pm: Killarney Lakes, Killarney

Frank Lewis
A PERFECT LANDING
8.00pm: Killarney, Co. Kerry

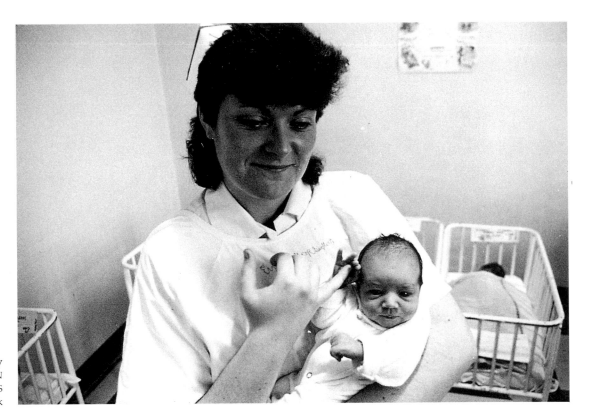

James Healy
IRELAND'S FUTURE IN
CARING HANDS
9.15pm: Erinville Hospital, Cork

Joe Healy
ST PATRICK'S BRIDGE
9.15pm: St Patrick's Bridge, Cork

Barney Champion
DUBLIN: THE FOUR COURTS
9.15pm: Dublin

Paul McFadden
GRIANAN OF AILEACH FORT
9.15pm: Burt, Co. Donegal

Tom Dunne
TIME FOR A CUPPA
11.35pm: Shanagolden,
Co. Limerick

Bernadette Madden
PATRICK MASON AT HOME
11.30pm: Airfield Road,
Rathgar, Dublin

The woman seems lost, as if the blue hoarding hides the street she once knew.
Someone has excluded her, and she wonders why.

NEIL JORDAN

This charming house in its deceptively pastoral setting proved irresistible to me. It lies close to the City Centre on a stretch of the Grand Canal beloved of the poet Patrick Kavanagh. Happily on a Saturday the place was free of traffic. It's part of my own neighbourhood and close to where my husband and I have our home and reared our five children. I feel a great pride and affection for the locality. Described by Maurice Craig as 'a suburb of enviable beauty', it's a neighbourhood which holds many happy memories for me, not least of these being the sheer pleasure and satisfaction of working with people actively interested in preserving the particular quality and charm of their environment.

THE RT. HON. THE LORD MAYOR
ALDERMAN CARMENCITA HEDERMAN

DUBLIN
The
MILLENNIUM

Thomas F. Byrne
BUSY BY DAY, BEAUTIFUL BY NIGHT
3.00am: Heuston Station

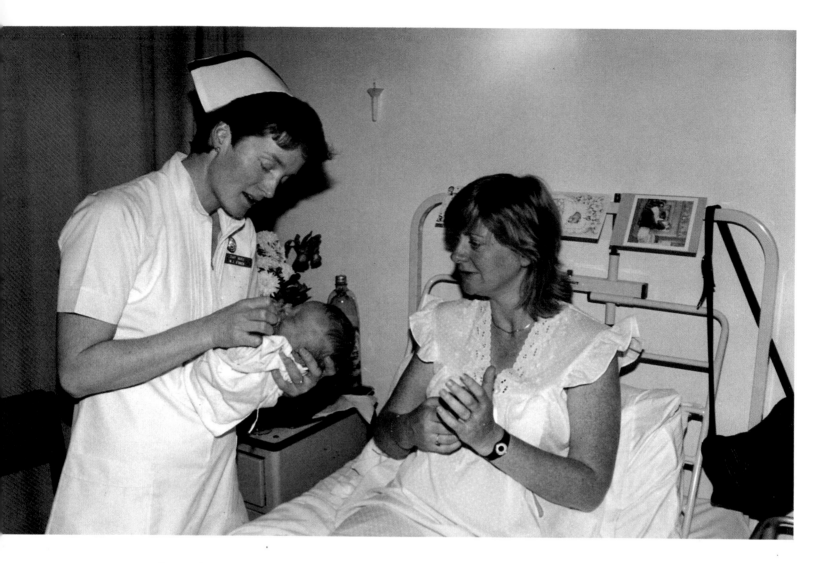

Seamus Smith
EARLY ARRIVAL
12.35am: National Maternity
Hospital